CHIL

COTIN

Chris Harris

Copyright © 1997 by Chris Harris

All rights reserved. No part of this book may be reproduced
or used in any form or by any means including graphic,
electronic, or mechanical without the prior written
permission of the publisher.

Edited by Darlene Calyniuk
Designed by Vic Marks
Typeset by The Typeworks, Vancouver, BC
Printed and bound in China

Canadian Cataloguing in Publication Data
    Harris, Chris, 1939–
    Chilcotin
        ISBN 0-9695235-6-4 (bound) — ISBN 0-9695235-7-2 (pbk.)
        1.Chilcotin River Region (BC)—Pictorial works. I. Title.
    FC3845.C445H37   1997   971.1'75   C97-910081-X
    F1089.C445H37   1997

The photograph on the front cover has been altered to facilitate the
title's composition. The original image can be seen on pp. 80–81.
No other images in this book have been computer enhanced or altered.

TITLE PAGE
Serenity at Dawn
WILDERNESS LAKE

PREVIOUS LEAF
Riding the Ridge
ABOVE CHILKO LAKE

RIGHT
Fly Fishing at Dusk
ATNARKO RIVER

Acknowledgements

Photography & Writing—Chris Harris
Picture Selection—Chris Harris, Vic Marks
Design—Vic Marks
Editing—Darlene Calyniuk
Typesetting—The Typeworks
Map Creation—Eric Leinberger

My sincere gratitude to the many wonderful Chilcotins whose friendship, hospitality, local expertise and regional knowledge provided me with opportunity and inspiration. Without their generous support, this book would not have been possible.

AIR SERVICES: Duncan Stewart of Tweedsmuir Air Services (Nimpo Lake), Dave and Mike King of White Saddle Air Services (Tatla Lake).

GUIDE OUTFITTERS: Connie & Alex and Gerry & Alf Bracewell of Bracewell's Alpine Wilderness Adventures; Joyce & David Dorsey of Rainbow Mountain Outfitters; Len Ellis of Bella Coola Outfitting; Karen, Corinne & Bud McLean and Ryan Schmidt of McLean's Ts'yl-os Park Lodge; Wanda & Roger Williams of Itcha-Ilgachuz Mountain Outfitters.

MODELS: Sheril & Samantha Mathews, Alex Bracewell, Amanda Kolk.

PHOTOGRAPHIC SUPPORT: Steve Good—Custom Color Labs; Uwe Mummenhoff—Lowepro; Allen Slade—Patagonia; Ken Smith—Cymbolic Sciences International.

PUBLICATION SUPPORT: Bill Bouchard—BC Ferries.

OTHERS: Debbie & Dave Altherr, Louis Bernollies, Peter Bueschkens, Doug Clarke, Julia Day, Caroline & Graeme Drew, Barb & Howard Gilbert, Mark Gilman, Brenda Gould, Phyllis & Donn Irwin, Lori ,Dave and Jen King, Randy Lavoie, Genny & Fraser MacLean, Brian McCutchen, Sally & Fritz Mueller, Karl Osmers, Bev & Larry Ramstad, Enubi & Petrus Rykes, Barrie Wall, Eve & Sam Whitehead, Karen Winsor & Paul Luft.

Many thanks to Vic Marks and his staff at The Typeworks for their knowledge and expertise with the layout and design of this book, and to Darlene Calyniuk, my editor, whose professional knowledge I sincerely appreciate.

Many thanks to close friends who continue to renew my zest for creative living and frontier discovery: Jim Boyde, Darlene & Mike Calyniuk, Tom Ellison, Dean Hull, Brenda and Jack Jenkins, Sheril Mathews who was a close companion on several photographic expeditions, and Jane & Tony O'Malley.

I would like to express my appreciation to BC Ferries (operators of the Discovery Coast Passage connecting Port Hardy on Vancouver Island to Bella Coola and the Chilcotin) for their generosity and support.

Flat Out
WILLIAMS LAKE STAMPEDE

A Few Words about the Chilcotin and Bella Coola Valley

The Chilcotin and Bella Coola Valley stretches 375 kilometers from Quesnel in the north to Lillooet in the south, and westward from the Fraser River's canyon walls near Williams Lake, towards the Central Pacific Coast fjordlands. Viewed and explored herein as a single region, this area of British Columbia is an unexpected treasure for explorers seeking respite and reward from the usual adventure destinations.

This region is an unparalleled study of contrasts, providing the most diverse opportunity for outdoor recreation found anywhere in British Columbia. The Fraser, Chilcotin and Chilko Rivers create huge sand dunes and towering hoodoos in the canyonlands. Rafting, birding, fishing and camping are recreational highlights. Westward, above these river canyons, stretches the dry Chilcotin Plateau. Here, in the rainshadow of the Coast Mountains, a mixture of open grasslands and lodgepole pine forests flourish, dotted by large and small lakes. The area is a playground for canoeists and kayakers, horseriders and wildlife viewers. Moving still westward from Tweedsmuir Park, the high glaciated peaks of the Coast Mountains give way to the Bella Coola Valley with its rainforests and rivers descending to the ocean. Here, hiking, fishing and wildlife viewing are exceptional.

The frontier characters who have shaped the cultural evolution of this area are as compelling as its fascinating topography. Resourceful Natives, Europeans and North Americans have endured the land's challenges and, together, have established their homes and shaped their communities. Today, through improved transportation along the Freedom Highway, the new BC Ferry service (connecting Bella Coola to Vancouver Island), and more frequent air service, the Chilcotin-Coast region is opening its doors to increased tourism. Timeless and untouched, the region holds untold delights for the traveler willing to step off the beaten path.

For information on the Chilcotin region of British Columbia, write to:

CARIBOO TOURISM ASSOCIATION
Box 4900, Williams Lake, BC
V2G 2V8 CANADA

CHILCOTIN MAP

PHOTO LOCATIONS

15 ► Photo page number

ELEVATION

■ 0 - 200 m.

■ 200 - 1,000 m.

■ 1,000 - 2,000 m.

■ 2,000 - 3,000 m.

▭ Glacier

------ B.C. Ferries

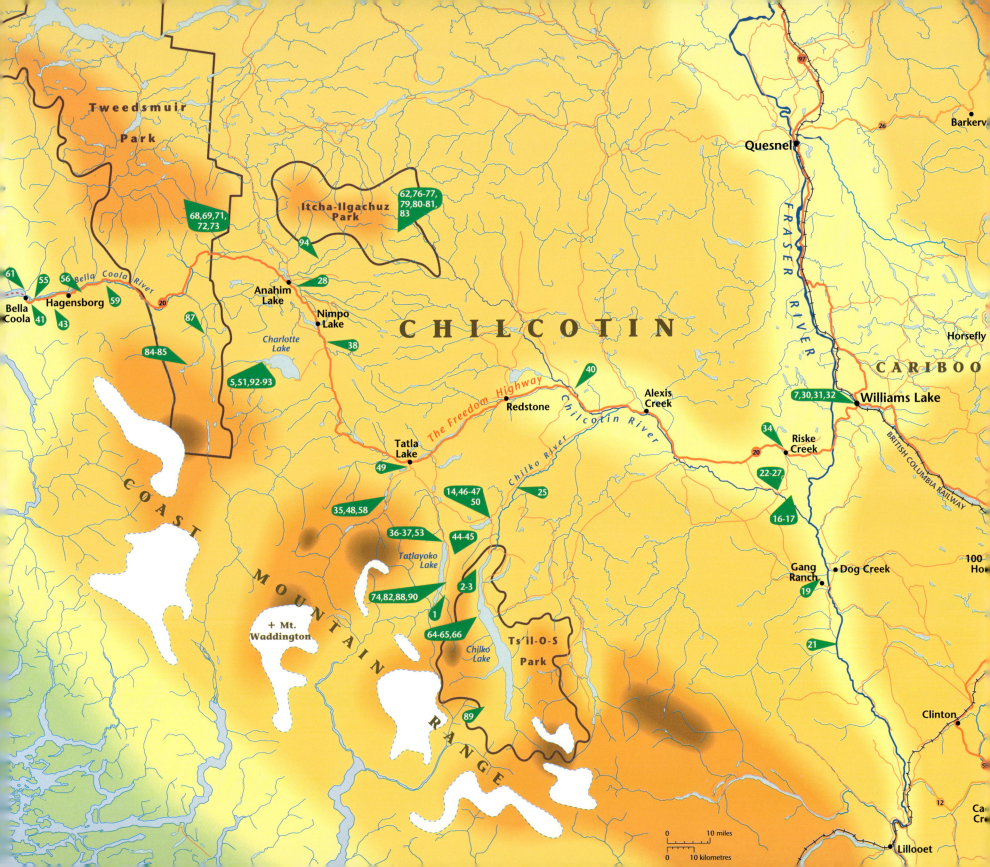

Author's Preface

The Chilcotin and Bella Coola Valley is a vast area to photograph in a short period of two summers. I vividly remember the first reconnaissance trip and the concern I had about achieving my goals. As I knew only three people, I went first to visit them. Amidst the warm welcome, I outlined my book project. Eagerly, they introduced me to their friends in key locations around the countryside. A few hours unfolded into a congenial week of getting a feel for the land. People were exceptionally friendly. When I first entered the Bella Coola Valley, I learned to drive with my hand on top of the steering wheel. Everyone says "good-day" by raising a couple of fingers from his wheel; no one goes unacknowledged. These subtle courtesies echo the Chilcotin spirit. By the week's end, I knew I had made lifetime friends. The adventure had begun!

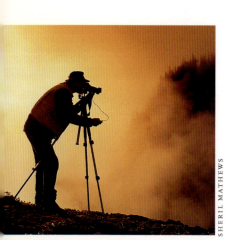

Author at work

My Ford Ranger with its "Bigfoot" camper acted as base camp when I wasn't on camping stints. Occasionally, a friend's driveway served as a late night sanctuary and the call "coffee is ready" was dawn's harbinger. Over time the "Bigfoot" became known to many and welcomed by all. I felt part of the Chilcotin family.

Adventure and exploration are delicately interwoven with the fabric of the Chilcotin people. Seemingly quiet 'still lifes' of the area speak passionately of the respect, honor and ingenuity of its people. An unattended roadside stand proudly displays organic produce. The rustic basket allows one to weigh his goods and then pay in the open tin receptacle. Without question one pays; without question the money stays.

Roadside Integrity

I dropped in to meet the McLeans at their resort on Chilko Lake. After listening to a few stories from Bud, I realized I was in the audience of an original settler. Bud, the pioneer, reveled in the challenges of early frontier life. So, it was with great surprise that I came to know the 'other Bud', the artist—author, director and film maker—through his extraordinarily professional one and a half hour production, *"Valley of the Grizzly"*. Nestled in the mountains of BC, polarities in talent unite. You never know in the Chilcotin!

Early another morning, I drove into the Tatlayoko Valley looking for Alex Bracewell. Mother Bracewell, Gerry, ordered me to sit down and join them for a

Going flat out

morning meal. Alf, her husband, soon appeared, grabbed the frying pan and promptly added a half pound of bacon and several eggs—a normal Chilcotin breakfast, I presumed. Later, with coffee in hand, he regaled me with road-building stories of the 1950s. Alf was one of the two bulldozer operators who touched blades on "The Hill" in 1952—a symbol of the completion of the road connecting Bella Coola with Williams Lake. Gerry's historic video footage is a testament to those hardy men who braved the dangers of early road construction; such dangers included crude blasting techniques and cat-driving on the edge of a thousand-foot vertical drop. In 1955, the highway was officially opened. This feat marked the first time the residents of Bella Coola had "a way out". Today, the road is known as the "Freedom Highway".

Gerry is an adventurer in her own right. She has been a guide-outfitter in the Tatlayoko Valley for over fifty years. I joined her on a horsepack trip through the Potato Mountains and was inspired by her sense of adventure. Midday, riding through the alpine flowers, I noticed a skyline ridge set against a clear blue sky. "Gerry," I asked sheepishly, "would you mind riding along that ridge so I could take a photograph?" "Ya-hoo!" was all I heard as she cantered off toward the ridge beckoning another rider to join her. With hardly enough time to dismantle and ready my camera, they were both galloping, flat out, across the ridge. Would you believe Gerry is 74 years old and still leading pack trips?

Vast areas, inaccessible by vehicle, make a flightseeing trip a necessity. From Bluff Lake near Tatla Lake, I flew with bush pilot Dave King, photographing spectacular panoramas. The verdant Tatlayoko and Chilko Lake valleys are not to be outdone by the Homathko Icefield and Mt. Waddington, the highest peak in the whole Coast Mountain Range. The Tiedemann Glacier leads up to the 4016 meter peak, first climbed in 1936. On another occasion, Duncan Stewart airlifted me over Hunlen Falls and the Turner Lakes from his resort on Nimpo Lake. While flying, potential photographs danced in my head. "Drop me and pick me up in four days!" I yelled. Within half an hour, I spotted several mountain goats and eagerly headed off. On a highly polished slab of granite I slipped, fell and broke my camera body. With my spare body (photographic, that is!) I headed out once again, remembering to slow down when hiking alone in a remote wilderness area. The accompanying photograph of five

Tiedemann Glacier

Five mountain goats

Solo expedition

Back to base camp

Family chores

mountain goats overlooking an iceberg-filled lake is keynote to four memorable days. Nascent territory, just half an hour off the highway, is evidence enough that the Chilcotin is BC's last frontier.

A physical challenge is just as engaging as a photographic one, so in March of 1996, I combined the two by heading into Tweedsmuir Park on a solo ski expedition. Temperatures to -30C, a sleigh in tow with heavy camping and photography equipment, and plenty of solitude gave me time to think and reassess the physical challenge for which I thought I longed! But without the lows, one wouldn't be aware of the highs. And what a reward! Five brilliant days of Coast Mountain vistas and clear cold moonlit nights. I am invigorated, I feel alive, and my senses are heightened.

A Rainbow Mountains horseback trip with Joyce, David and Leslie Dorsey, came to a close with an invitation to their home for a winter weekend. They promised moose sightings. Never before had I felt the romance of frontier life as I did on this occasion. At the end of a long, remote, wintry road I was met by snowmobiles pulling sleighs. I loaded my gear, and off we went into the cold Chilcotin wilderness. Their home had no power or running water: it felt wonderfully simple. In the morning light, coyotes crossed the fields and moose fed on hay alongside the horses. Later in the day, Dave harnessed up his team of Percheron horses, attached a flat-bottomed sleigh, and we rode to a tall spruce forest in search of wood. On that crisp, cold and clear day, the distinctive jingling sound of harness buckles and sleigh runners squeaking over frozen snow brought back the distant memories of Dr. Zhivago's romantic Siberian countryside. A candlelight supper and a sauna under a -25C starlit sky rounded out the magical day.

Romance and adventure abound in this, British Columbia's last frontier. During the past two years I have endeavored to capture the essence of the Chilcotin and Bella Coola Valley. Enjoy the results, and if possible, explore the region and meet the locals yourselves. You'll never regret this adventure.

CHRIS HARRIS

CHILCOTIN

A Photographic Portrayal

The Grasslands

Formed in the rainshadow of the Coast Mountains, the Chilcotin grasslands evolved some thirteen million years ago in climates characterized by cold winters and hot summers. More recently, grassland areas are being threatened, and even though they appear to stretch on forever, they probably represent more of an "endangered space" than old growth forests in British Columbia.

Scattered over the grasslands are many depressions left by glaciers. Now fed by streams, these depressions become the lakes and marshes that punctuate the Chilcotin grasslands, transforming it into one of the most prolific waterfowl regions in British Columbia. Eared Grebes and Barrow's Goldeneyes are among the unique summer inhabitants.

For those with a camera, the grasslands are often a challenge to photograph. Their seemingly indistinctive quality demands sensitivity to detail. To the perceptive eye, compelling compositions evolve through color, shapes, lines, textures and perspective. The world within animates. Slowly, the open grasslands take on a definitive character.

Autumn Leaves

SPLIT-RAIL RUSSELL FENCE

The Way Home
CHILCOTIN GRASSLANDS

LEFT
Grasslands Forever
CHILCOTIN GRASSLANDS

Nature Viewing

The Grasslands and Canyonlands comprise very little of the Chilcotin region, yet support more flora and fauna than any other habitat. The area is a treasure trove to the avid naturalist. Wildflowers include Arrowleaf Balsam Root, Big Sagebrush and Prickly Pear Cactus; sun loving insects such as the Caroline grasshopper, the Alpine butterfly, wasps and bees also flourish here. And with the insects come the birds. For the bird lover there is a variety of rare bats, hawks, eagles, owls and woodpeckers. Long-billed Curlews, Meadowlarks, Vesper Sparrows and Horned Larks are among the select populace which feeds or nests in the open grasslands. The Tundra Swan, American White Pelican (see inset photo) and Canada Goose also take momentary refuge migrating to nesting grounds beyond. Truly, these areas combine for a world class nature viewing opportunity.

Rolling Hills
GANG RANCH

Grasslands and Canyons
MID-FRASER CANYON

Desert Sunrise

FARWELL CANYON

High Adventure
CHILKO RIVER

The Canyonlands

The Canyonlands of the Chilko, Chilcotin and Fraser Rivers are very special places. Gouged out through time and erosion, the steep cliffs of lava rock, limestone and clay form impressive landscapes. Narrow ledges, crevices, talus slopes and silt beaches speak of a time gone by and now provide homes and feeding grounds for a variety of birds and animals. The cliff walls not only furnish safe, secure homes, but also warm and cozy ones. They soak up the sun's heat all day and release it slowly, during the night, providing a warm microclimate. White-throated Swifts, Rock Wrens and Rosy Finches use these high limestone cliffs for shelter; bats roost in the crevices on hot, summer days. During the evenings, some wildlife feeds on moths in the forests above the cliffs, while others descend to the sagebrush by the rivers to hunt insects.

Bald and Golden Eagles hunt above the canyon walls, while California Bighorn sheep, mule deer, coyote, fox, Black bear and cougar slip down to the shores in need of water.

Veins of Sand
FARWELL CANYON

Farwell Canyon

A breathtaking spectacle is Farwell Canyon situated just west of Williams Lake and south of Riske Creek. Even from one's vehicle are visible the huge limestone "hoodoos" towering above the Chilcotin River. A short hike above these hoodoos takes you to an 'active' sand dune. With

everchanging light, sand dunes are an exciting environment to photograph (refer to page 22). Keep your eyes open for California Bighorn sheep which travel the steep cliffs below. At breaktime, watch where you sit. The hot arid land is the perfect environment for the small prickly pear cactus!

The Freedom Highway

Originally known as the Freedom Road, Highway 20 stretches 452 kilometers from Williams Lake to Bella Coola. In British Columbia, this was the third road to reach the Pacific. The route includes both paved and gravel sections, and is most famous because of "The Hill"—a drop of 1400 meters from Tweedsmuir Park to the Bella Coola Valley. Although there are no traffic lights along the entire route, you may well be forced to stop for cattle, moose or bear.

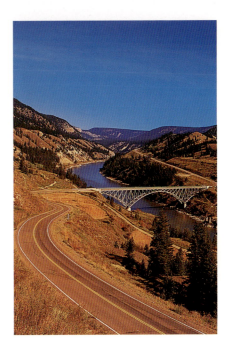

Traveling west from Williams Lake, the crossing of Sheep Creek Bridge, with its spectacular view of the Fraser River Canyon, officially marks the entrance to the Chilcotin. The climb to the 1200 meter-high Chilcotin Plateau chronicles where the earliest ranchers in the area settled. At Riske Creek you can head south to Farwell Canyon and the Gang Ranch, or further west at Hanceville you can travel south to the Nemaiah Valley and Ts'yl-os Park. At kilometer 111 is Alexis Creek, the first major service center with RCMP and Red Cross stations.

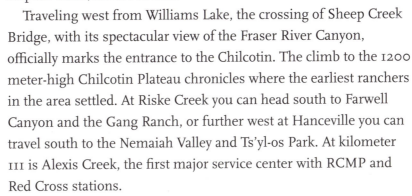

After traveling through Bull Canyon and past the Chilanko Marsh Wildlife Viewing Area, Tatla Lake emerges with its spectacular views of the glaciated Coast Mountains. From Tatla Lake, one can head south into three magnificent mountain valleys—the Bluff Lake, Tatlayoko Lake and Chilko Lake Valleys. Outdoor recreation opportunities abound here.

Next along the highway are the towns of Nimpo Lake and Anahim Lake. There are many holiday resorts in this region where fishing claims an international reputation. Nimpo Lake is known as the float plane capital of British Columbia. Air charters to fly-in fishing cabins and remote recreation locations are encouraged here.

Still westward from Anahim Lake is Tweedsmuir Park, famous for its Rainbow Range, Alexander Mackenzie Heritage Trail, Hunlen Falls and Turner Lake canoe route. Now is the time to descend "The Hill" to the Bella Coola Valley and the towns of Hagensborg and Bella Coola. Here, recreational and cultural activities are renowned.

In 1996, BC Ferries commenced "The Discovery Coast Passage" connecting Bella Coola to Port Hardy on Vancouver Island. This new circle route provides endless opportunities for sightseeing and adventure.

Chilcotin Bound

PREVIOUS LEFT
Solo Challenge
WILLIAMS LAKE STAMPEDE

PREVIOUS RIGHT
Speed and Skill
WILLIAMS LAKE STAMPEDE

LEFT
Team Effort
WILLIAMS LAKE STAMPEDE

LEFT
Abandoned Dream
FREEDOM HIGHWAY

Early Settler
CHILCOTIN BACKROAD

"The Hill"

Since the early 1900s, Bella Coola citizens have struggled to get a road out of the Valley to the Chilcotin Plateau, Williams Lake and beyond. For years only packhorse trails provided access to the outside world.

In the 1930s and again in the 1940s the Bella Coola Board of Trade petitioned the government's Department of Highways, but again and again the idea was repeatedly refused. The Provincial authorities did not believe that a third road to the Pacific over the Coast Mountains merited consideration—too expensive for so few people. Finally, in the 1950s, the citizens of Bella Coola decided to take action. The Board of Trade sent a telegram to the Department of Public Works in Victoria: "This is to advise you that we are going to immediately start building the road from Anahim Lake to Bella Coola".

The major obstacle was the precipitous "hill" which descended approximately 1,666 meters from Heckman Pass—the highest point on the highway—to the ocean. So with supplies bought on credit and nothing more than promises of being paid, Elijah Gurr with the help of Thomas Squinas, a native wolf hunter, found and blazed the best route for the road. In September of 1952, with Alf Bracewell and George Dalshaug at the controls, two bulldozers began their assault. When asked about the construction crew, Alf said, "The whole crew was a cat operator, a swamper and a cook—no boss or nothin'." By working long hours and taking great chances, the two construction crews carved a road through the side of a rock mountain. By September 1953 the two cats were less than a mile apart. At this point, promised wages were of little concern as the two crews raced towards one another. Spectators, including Alf's wife, Gerry, with a video camera, gathered to watch the uniting of east and west. With the final boulders being pushed aside, the two cats with blades lowered, touched on September 26, 1953. "The Freedom Road" had been completed, and the citizens of Bella Coola finally had a "way out".

Today, "The Hill" is still the only land route in and out of the Valley. Even with its 18% grade, single lane sections and gravel switchbacks, the road is traveled daily by all kinds of motor vehicles, including semi-trailers.

PREVIOUS LEAF
Mountain Reflections
TATLAYOKO LAKE

LEFT
Test of Time
EAST OF NIMPO LAKE

Native Petroglyph

My evening meanderings led me through a lush and entangled rainforest and into the ancient ceremonial world of the Nuxalk Nations—a site with over 100 rock carvings. According to anthropologists, this remote location was known only to the Chiefly, Noble and Supernatural Secret Societies. Here, they kept their "spirit power" and dealt with "supernatural matters." The mystical tranquility and powerful divinity of the site is captured in the face of this primordial petroglyph.

Native Graveyard: Redstone
FREEDOM HIGHWAY

Morning Mist

BELLA COOLA RIVER

Bella Coola Valley

The Bella Coola Valley is believed to have been first inhabited by Native peoples some ten thousand years ago. Their villages were located along the banks of the Bella Coola, Dean and Noeich Rivers. There they settled because of the resources: easy transportation, fresh water, fish and berries

and medicinal plants. Also of great importance were cedar trees. Planks for building houses, dugout canoes, clothing, mats and baskets were woven from cedar bark. A resourceful people, the Natives became hunters, fishermen and traders. Today, descendants from all the early village sites live in the town of Bella Coola as part of the Nuxalk First Nation.

Contact with the outside world began with fur traders in the late 1600s, and by 1793 Alexander Mackenzie arrived in Bella Coola by land. One hundred years later, having suffered a severe economic depression in the United States, a group of Norwegians arrived from Minnesota to establish a settlement. Here they became the first commercial loggers, fishermen and farmers. Restorations have recently begun to preserve examples of their square-timbered buildings. A striking replica of this Norwegian influence is Barb's Pottery Shop. The center of their community was what is now the town of Hagensborg—about 20 kilometers east of Bella Coola.

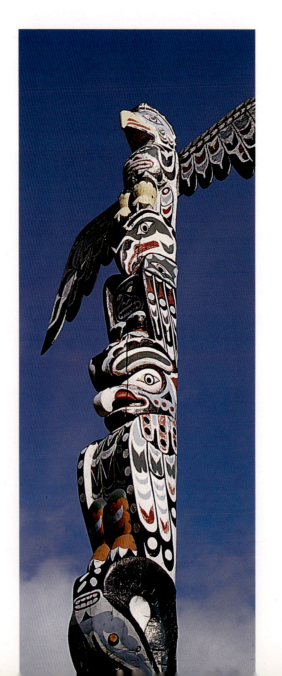

PREVIOUS LEAF
Golden Sunrise
TATLAYOKO LAKE

LEFT
A Day's Work is Done
CHILCOTIN RUSSELL FENCE

Hay Harvest

KING'S RANCH

Mother Nature

TATLA LAKE

LEFT
Imperial Dawn
CHOELQUOIT LAKE

Mystical Morning
LITTLE CHARLOTTE LAKE

Cast Away
TATLAYOKO LAKE

The Rainforest

800 Years Old
BELLA COOLA VALLEY

The temperate rainforest rises up from the western slopes of the Coast Mountains in Bella Coola Valley. The undergrowth, characterized by Devil's Club, Salmonberry, and curtains of moss draping from huge branches, lends a lushness to this spectral growth.

With heavy winter rains and a mild winter season, these trees grow year round, live for centuries, and reach immense sizes. Within the Big Cedar Tree Recreational Site, established by the BC Forest Service, reigns a Western Red Cedar tree five meters in diameter. So large, it merits formal registration in Victoria, the province's capital. This rainforest is one of the most biologically productive environments on earth.

The Nuxalk people, who have lived in the Valley for hundreds of years, depended upon the abundance of the forest for their food, homes, totem poles and canoes. The woodsmen among them used stone axes and cedar root ropes to drag their logs. The Norwegian colonists, having arrived in the 1890s, became the next generation of loggers who used crosscut saws, springboards and axes. Close scrutiny of old stumps reflects a time gone by with springboard holes and remnants of old crosscut saws.

My Grizzly Bear Story!

The Chilcotin and Bella Coola Valley is grizzly country. My patience for an opportunity to photograph the bear was growing thin. I headed down to the Bella Coola River where I knew Grizzly bears would be "reeling in" on the fall salmon run. The early evening light near Tweedsmuir Lodge shrouded a Grizzly mom with two cubs. "Perfect," I said to myself. "I'll be back at sunrise." At daybreak, with my bear spray at-the-ready on my belt, I headed along a trail one hundred meters above the river where the vantage point was all. Without warning, the bellow of a bear broke the morning silence. Two cubs scampered down the trail ahead of me and almost instantly a Grizzly sow assumed "standoff" position eight meters directly in front of me. My shaking hand failed to find the bear spray. She tensed, reared up, growled, then charged. No chance for prayer. I threw my precious camera and tripod up the trail towards her, lowered my eyes, and fumbled for the spray. When I looked up, the Grizzly had halted four meters in front of me, turned, and roared off after her cubs. I lost the photographic opportunity, but somehow I still got the 'bigger picture'. I gave thanks for the power of 'mother love'.

Scampering Cub
BELLA COOLA VALLEY

Beyond Bella Coola

Beyond Bella Coola lies British Columbia's Mid-Coast. With over a thousand islands within, it's an immense expanse of snow-topped peaks, narrow valleys and fjords. The Mid-Coast contains eight different biogeoclimatic zones and is home to the coastal rainforest, rare wildlife and an abundance of plant species.

In May 1996, BC Ferries expanded its service to the Mid-Coast from Bella Coola to Port Hardy on Vancouver Island, adding additional stops at Ocean Falls, Klemtu, Bella Bella, Namu and Finn Bay. Recreational opportunities abound throughout the region, drawing North Americans as well as Europeans for steelhead and salmon fishing, kayaking and scuba diving, wildlife viewing and mountain climbing. Little wonder BC Ferries calls this "The Discovery Coast Passage."

PREVIOUS LEFT
Yellow Hues
BLUFF LAKE ROAD

PREVIOUS RIGHT
Verdant Forest
MOUNTAIN STREAM

Fisherman's Sanctuary
BELLA COOLA HARBOUR

Chilcotin Plateau

After crossing Sheep Creek Bridge above the Fraser River, and heading west along the Freedom Highway, one climbs 1200 meters to where a vast Chilcotin panorama unfolds. This is the Chilcotin Plateau.

Over two million years ago, an effusion of lava seeped through vents and flowed over the low lying areas of the Chilcotin creating a plateau. During the last ice age meltdown, massive chunks of ice broke off receding glaciers. The weight from these formed depressions which later became 'kettle' lakes. Today, grasslands surround the kettle lakes creating extensive grazing areas for homesteads such as the Gang Ranch.

Across the Plateau, cattle forage behind split-rail Russell fences and bluebirds flit in and out of nesting boxes. Salmon and trout run the rivers while large populations of moose, deer, Bighorn sheep, mountain goats and Black and Grizzly bears roam the wilderness.

Endless Vista
TOWARD TWEEDSMUIR PARK

Southern Exposure

CHILKO LAKE

PREVIOUS LEAF
Wonderment
CHILKO AND TSUNIAH LAKES

"The Chilcotin Way"

I had met Alex Bracewell in the Tatlayoko Valley. His response to my book project was immediate and enthusiastic: "I have a group of Swiss clients arriving for a remote wilderness horse packtrip through the mountains. I need to clear the trail, so, if you're willing to work as well as photograph, I'll show you the *real* Chilcotin." I jumped at the opportunity and we were on our way within the week. We trail blazed from dawn to dusk; a ten-day trip compacted into three. Our trek took us south from Bracewell's Lodge, around the southern end of Tatlayoko Lake, and then north again above the lake's western side. As we rode and worked our way through spectacular mountain scenery, I often wondered how would we get back across the lake to the lodge. Not wanting to appear "a greenhorn", I never asked. During those three days we worked hard, laughed hardy, and slept well. Eventually our descent took us from the mountains to the lake. I was about to discover the extended meaning of ingenious. A lopsided raft (Alex had tacked together) lay tethered to a tree in a small bay. Without breaking stride, our horses and gear were aboard and we pushed off. The accompanying photograph shows Captain Alex ferrying his raft three kilometers back to his lodge. While I was pondering 'how' and 'why', Alex's resourcefulness answered 'how about' and 'why not'. To Alex, no challenge is so great that a little Chilcotin ingenuity can't provide the answers. It's just "The Chilcotin Way"!

Time and Erosion
RAINBOW MOUNTAINS

Ribbons of Color
RAINBOW MOUNTAINS

Adventures by Horse

The sheer magnitude of the Chilcotin landscape—distances and colors—is truly breathtaking. The best way to explore these mountain ranges is by horseback with guide outfitters whose families have been scouring their respective areas for generations. What better way to learn about the local history and land formations than by chatting around the campfire with a genuine 'old-timer.' The inset photos show views of the Coast Mountain range and an alpine meadow of wild potatoes in bloom. The volcanic Rainbow and Itcha-Ilgachuz Mountains (photos pp. 72, 73, 76–77, 79, 80–81) hint at the turbulent beginning and sensuous erosion of the landscape. Too much to internalize in one outing, this area bears exploring again and again.

RIGHT
Roundup at Dawn
TWEEDSMUIR PARK

OVERLEAF LEFT
Chromatic Harmony
RAINBOW MOUNTAINS

OVERLEAF RIGHT
Volcanic Validity
RAINBOW MOUNTAINS

Fishing

The Chilcotin and Bella Coola Valley are world renowned fishing destinations. On the Plateau, Nimpo Lake is known as the floatplane capital of British Columbia. From here, a tranquil wilderness cabin and guaranteed quality fishing beckon. The opportunity to catch "wild rainbow" is unique in the province. These indigenous trout have existed here historically with no interference from introduced strains. Also, the less prolific rainbow have never had to compete with salmon which cannot climb up over the Coast Range. Nowadays, with catch and release and the resulting low mortality rate, sportfishing in the area has great promise for years to come.

Both in the Bella Coola Valley and the fjordlands beyond, fishing is excellent. In the Valley, anglers can fish the Bella Coola, Atnarko and Lower Dean Rivers for steelhead, dolly varden, whitefish, rainbow and cutthroat trout, and spring and coho salmon. For salt water fishing, charter boats and guides can be hired at the Bella Coola wharf; fish for salmon, halibut and cod, or trap crab and dig for clams.

Last Frontier

TOWARD THE COAST MOUNTAINS

Canoeing and Hiking

If you're looking for a challenging adventure, the West Chilcotin and the Bella Coola Valley abound with canoeing and hiking opportunities.

In the Valley, the BC Forest Service provides detailed hiking pamphlets of the area's numerous trails. Some of the shorter treks highlight points overlooking the whole Bella Coola Valley and coastal fjords beyond, while longer hikes explore the alpine nestled amongst glaciers and snow-capped peaks.

The most famous trail is the Alexander Mackenzie Heritage Trail which stretches 420 kilometers from near Quesnel to Bella Coola. This route traces prehistoric Carrier Indian trader routes to Tweedsmuir Park and down to Bella Coola. The park section through the Rainbow Range is as varied as it is breathtaking.

For canoe enthusiasts, eager for a wilderness setting, the Turner Lake Chain in Tweedsmuir Park provides clear water, excellent fishing and unrivaled mountain scenery. The chain includes seven lakes, sandy beaches and short portages. To enjoy the trip, allow four to seven days—more if the plan is to hike some of the spectacular trails up to the alpine.

PREVIOUS LEAF
Pack Train
ITCHA MOUNTAINS

Shadowlight
ITCHA MOUNTAINS

PREVIOUS LEAF
Nature's Artistry
MT. FUKAWI

LEFT & RIGHT
Chilcotin Time
IN THE MOUNTAINS

Hunlen Falls

Hunlen Falls, at the northern end of Turner Lake, is Canada's third highest free falling waterfalls at over 360 meters. You can visit the falls by flying in from Nimpo Lake, or by hiking the 16.4 kilometer Hunlen Trail. The trail starts at the Atnarko Tote Road near the bottom of "The Hill" and follows old Indian routes, including that of the Indian trapper, Hana-Lin, for whom Hunlen Falls is named. The trail includes over seventy-five switch-backs, climbs over two thousand meters, and is a seven- to nine-hour hike. That it is prime Grizzly bear habitat adds even a greater challenge.

Upon reaching Turner Lake, the trail crosses a footbridge at the narrows above the falls—an excellent place to fly-fish. Further on, paralleling the southeast wall of Hunlen Creek Canyon, a lush, lichen-laden forest produced by the continual mist rising from the falls, adds mystery and magic to the area. Be careful, the sheer drop-offs and crumbling edges make this both an exhilarating and potentially dangerous setting.

PREVIOUS LEAF
Symmetry in Motion
JUNKER LAKE

RIGHT
Ocean Bound
HUNLEN FALLS

Ridge Riders
OVER TATLAYOKO LAKE

RIGHT
Aerial Pastels
COAST MOUNTAINS

LEFT
Repose and Replenish
TATLAYOKO LAKE AND COAST MOUNTAINS

OVERLEAF
Sacred Solitude
LITTLE CHARLOTTE LAKE

Our Responsibility

Experiencing the Chilcotin and Bella Coola Valley was the realization of a personal dream.

Remote wilderness, dramatic beauty, sparse population and unbridled freedom: the attraction of the Chilcotin to early explorers still rings true to modern adventurers. But with exploration comes the potential of unintentional exploitation. Paradoxically, rich in the natural resources of timber, minerals and spectacular beauty, the area is in danger of being destroyed by that which has made it flourish. Excessive resource extraction is already being questioned. Increased tourism also brings concern over depletion of natural resources and lifestyle. Too often we compromise our future in the name of progress. So how will human presence determine the Chilcotin's fate?

We British Columbians have an ongoing responsibility to be aware of issues challenging our frontiers. With this knowledge, our commitment to the preservation of these natural treasures must be unconditional. The Chilcotin (and Bella Coola Valley) must remain relatively undisturbed for the enjoyment and discovery of future generations. This is the dream I hope will be shared.

CHRIS HARRIS
February 1997
108 Mile Ranch, British Columbia

LEFT
Pioneer Spirit
CHILCOTIN WILDERNESS

"DISCOVER BRITISH COLUMBIA"®
Book, Card & Print Series

Through the *"Discover British Columbia"®* book, card and print series, Chris presents the opportunity to explore or revisit unique areas of BC, to marvel at and reflect upon their natural beauty, and to honor and appreciate the necessity of preserving this heritage.

The following four books have been published by Country Light Publishing and Chris Harris Photography. You can purchase these from your local bookstore or order autographed copies by contacting:

COUNTRY LIGHT PUBLISHING
Box 333–108 Mile Ranch
British Columbia, Canada, V0K 2Z0
Tel: 250-791-6631   Fax: 250-791-6671
1-800-946-6622
e-mail: harrisc@netshop.net

THE BOWRON LAKES

British Columbia's Wilderness Canoe Circuit is a photographic portrayal of "one of the top 10 canoe trips in the world" (*Outside Magazine*). This unique natural circuit of lakes and interconnecting waterways is situated in a wildlife sanctuary amidst the snow-capped Cariboo Mountains.

ISBN 0-9695235-0-5 $24.95 (soft cover)

CARIBOO COUNTRY

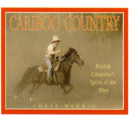

British Columbia's Spirit of the West is a photographic portrayal of the region's western heritage. It's a land which offers a magic and beauty stunning in its diversity.

ISBN 0-9695235-3-X $26.95 (soft cover)
ISBN 0-9695235-4-8 $36.95 (hard cover)

BC RAIL

British Columbia's Great Train Adventure captures the sense of exploration, excitement and romance along a 1,000-mile journey which encompasses some of the most spectacular and varied scenery in British Columbia.

ISBN 0-9695235-1-3 $24.95 (soft cover)
ISBN 0-9695235-2-1 $34.95 (hard cover)

CHILCOTIN

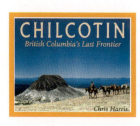

British Columbia's Last Frontier. Born out of volcanic activity and weathered by erosion, the physical and human landscapes of the Chilcotin Plateau and Bella Coola Valley have a color and composition unparalleled anywhere in BC. This photographic portrayal captures that energy and enchantment.

ISBN 0-9695235-7-2 $26.95 (soft cover)
ISBN 0-9695235-6-4 $36.95 (hard cover)